Fractured by Cattails
The Haiku Society of America
2023 Members' Anthology

Allyson Whipple
Editor

Haiku Society of America
New York

Fractured by Cattails

Copyright © 2023 by Haiku Society of America

Upon publication, all rights revert to the authors and artist.

ISBN: 978-1-930172-22-7

Cover artwork: Scott Wiggerman

Design: Allyson Whipple

Layout: Ed Vincent

Dedicated to the memory of
Ignatius Fay and his priceless contributions to
the Haiku Society of America

Introduction

One of the things I find most satisfying in my creative life is having the ability to showcase the work of my fellow poets. While I started writing because I wanted my own audience, as I got older, I became more interested in opportunities to create community. Before COVID, I ran my own poetry festival for two years, hosted readings and salons, and generally took whatever opportunity I could to create events and artifacts that brought people together. A pandemic and cross-country move later, I haven't lost that desire to make publications, podcast, and parties. So when Bryan Rickert asked me to take on the 2023 anthology, of course I said yes.

While Bryan cautioned me about the challenges that come with a themed anthology, the fact remains that I'm interested in building books that have a level of cohesion. Still, I knew that many in our organization prefer not to be confined by thematic constraints. I chose *elements* as the theme because it could be applied in the concrete and the abstract, the esoteric and the scientific. Poets could take inspiration from the classical elements that appear in various historical traditions (Greek, Vedic, Chinese), the period table, or abstractions such as the element of the surprise. I encouraged everyone to interpret the topic broadly, and you rose to the occasion.

Out of 430 submissions, most focused on the ancient Greek elements of fire, earth, water, and air. When I printed out the full set of selected poems, I quickly realized that there was nonetheless enough diversity that I couldn't easily divide sections into these four elements, with a miscellaneous section at the end. After a few rounds of reading and attempting to organize the manuscript, I eventually did away with sections altogether.

The fact is that however we interpret the elements, they do not exist in isolation. You cannot make fire without wood (or other earth materials) and air. Molecules require at least two atoms from the period table in order to exist; we can't get water without hydrogen and oxygen (both of which also are part of the molecular mixture of air). And because the abstract generally follows the concrete, we wouldn't have our metaphorical approach to elements if we didn't have physical elements to work from as a starting point.

Whether we are being literal or metaphorical, elements exist in a state of interdependency. In recognition of the ways in which all things are connected, I chose to do away with the section breaks entirely. And while the poems skewed heavily in one poetic direction, I have done my best to include a balance of the esoteric, the scientific, and the metaphorical on each page.

The title of this year's anthology comes from Kristen Lindquist's haiku, which can be found on the last page. I had a long list of potential titles that drew from selected haiku; it was tough to make a decision. However, I felt that having a generic title like "Elements" would do a disservice to the excellent range of poems in this anthology. I ultimately selected Lindquist's line because the haiku incorporates many elements at once. The haiku itself is a compelling concrete image. The line I chose also reminds me of impressionist and abstract expressionist paintings, as well as the representational stained glass windows found in the Dana Thomas House (designed by Frank Lloyd Wright) in Springfield, Illinois. The line is both concrete and abstract; it's representational without didactic. After many rounds of elimination, *fractured by cattails* best embodied the underlying aesthetic quality I wanted for this anthology.

I would like to thank Ed Vincent for donating his time to handle the anthology formatting. We would have a much less attractive anthology without him!

Thanks also to Scott Wiggerman for allowing us to use his collage *Totem* as our cover art, as well as for going to the trouble of getting a high-resolution scan *after* he'd already sold it! I chose this piece for the cover art because the interplay of colors and shapes illustrated what I wanted to achieve with this anthology: something bold, but not too didactic or representational. It speaks to something elemental without having overt meaning.

Finally, thank you to my fellow HSA board members who helped answer all of my institutional questions, and to the general membership for sending their work. I appreciate your faith in me as an editor!

Allyson Whipple
St. Louis, Missouri

at the wake
too little was made
out of *nothing*
    Juan Edgardo De Pascuale
    Gambier, Ohio

cold soup
a Boltzmann brain
thinks I am
    Roland Packer[1]
    Hamilton, Ontario

wolf moon
chipping mud
from my boots
    Kathy Goldbach
    Campbell, California

hand to hand
the softness
of a silver coin
    Tom Clausen
    Ithaca, New York

taking out the trash
   for fifty years —
  so much star-gazing
    Suzanne Niedzielska
    Glastonbury, Connecticut

bowing
to the harvest moon
sunflowers
  Denise Fontaine-Pincince
  Belchertown, Massachusetts

heavy rain
the pillow shuffle
at dawn
  Joanna Ashwell
  Durham, United Kingdom

clarsach concert —
in a ring of lanterns
winter wood
  Xenia Tran[2]
  Nairn, United Kingdom

a blush of holly
the come-hither strut
of the doe
    Diane Wallihan
    Port Townsend, Washington

    fossil hunting
    we find what we couldn't
    in the clouds
        Richard L. Matta
        San Diego, California

    turvy in the snow globe theatre of the absurd
        Maxianne Berger
        Outremont, Montreal

    cold front
    the dogwood soldiers on
    to spring
        Beverly Acuff Momoi[3]
        Mountain View, California

a bee and i
reach for the same peony
May day
    Susan B. Auld
    Buffalo Grove, Illinois

    hummingbirds at my window
    frenzy of green
    coffee brewing
        Kathryn Pumphrey
        Lynchburg, Virginia

    hot tea and egg rolls
    an Auschwitz survivor
    talks of UFOs
        Howard Lee Kilby
        Hot Springs National Park, Arkansas

    wrought iron railing
    the rust that came
    with the house
        Barrie Levine[4]
        Wenham, Massachusetts

puzzle pieces with
a haphazard fit...
mother's kintsugi
    Emily Rademacher
    Crystal Lake, Illinois

slow summer rain...
trying to pick the numbers
at Keno
    Bonnie Stepenoff
    Chesterfield, Missouri

the click of game tiles
on linoleum
all night moon
    Michelle Schaefer
    Bothwll, Washington

spring rabbit, rabbit
the pennycress fairies
whisper in the grass
    Anette Chaney
    Harrison, Arkansas

an old flame
darkness closing in
on a lump of wax
   Richard Tice[5]
   Kent, Washington

first love
a taste of sky
in the snowflake
   Marilyn Appl Walker[6]
   Madison, Georgia

Ocotillo canes
between the thorns
his touch
   Judith Morrison Schallberger
   San Jose, California

asking the world for a night off new moon
   Mike Rehling
   Presque Isle, Michigan

foghorn
floating somewhere
thirty tons of ore
    Marsh Muirhead
    Bemidji, Minnesota

    huddled over
    a steaming grate
    full moon
        Eric Tanner
        Sacramento, California

        his bluster
        the weather-vane spins
        on the red barn rooftop
            Joan Fingon
            Ventura, California

    above the train tracks
    skeleton tree waits
    for lightning
        Marcie Flinchum Atkins
        Fairfax, VA

baby birds
every sky starts
from the ground
   Brad Bennett
   Arlington, Massachusetts

   wood piling—
   the night heron lifts off
   changing the darkness
      Patricia J. Machmiller[8]
      San Jose, California

      painted air
      the sun's brushstroke
      unparalleled
         Christa Pandey
         Austin, Texas

   naturalist talk
   the layers of earth
   on his pants
      Annette Makino
      Arcata, California

on fire
the monk remains
in lotus position
   Frank Higgins
   Kansas City, Missouri

     mountain top
     the wind reaches
     further into me
        petro c.k.
        Seattle, Washington

          one more layer
          on the cast iron skillet...
          gloaming walk
              William O'Sullivan[9]
              Washington, D.C.

       thunder
       in a cloudless sky
       the storm within
          Valorie Broadhurst Woerdehoff
          Dubuque, Iowa

without
my consent
pond reflection
    Kelly Sargent[10]
    Williston, Vermont

    dust devil may care tumbleweed
        Eavonka Ettinger
        Long Beach, California

    Trees spread their fingers
    To the empty, white sky
    In stillness so can I
        Monica Lajoie
        Manchester, New Hampshire

a change in the air
she shows herself
plum blossoms
    Marylin Fleming
    Pewaukee, Wisconsin

monochrome marsh grass at dawn
   Jill Kessler
   Bluffton, South Carolina

A straight contrail slides
Like scissors slitting chiffon
Cutting through the clouds
   Deborah Troner
   Palmetto Bay, Florida

after the Dog's ears
perk up around the campfire,
—come to attention
   Jon Hanzen
   Pahoa, Hawaii

earth warming
my grandson's stories
begin with remember when
   MJ Mello
   Carolina, Rhode Island

false advertising—
more copy than nickel
in a nickel
   Wilda Morris
   Bolingbrook, Illinois

   forgetting I'm on an island Brooklyn sun
   Daniel Shank Cruz
   Jersey City, New Jersey

   TV Yule log
   a proposal
   with a cubic zirconia
     Lisa Sparaco
     Pearland, Texas

   distant mirage
   a merganser's flank
   flashed white
     Michael Sheffield
     Santa Rosa, California

equinox moonrise a neat part in the sea
    Matthew Caretti
    Mercersburg, Pennsylvania

in her eighties
she forgives it all —
falling leaves
    Penny Harter
    Mays Landing, New Jersey

unlikely truth
a milkweed pod
cracks open
    Sondra J. Byrnes
    Santa Fe, New Mexico

birthday morning
poking in the fireplace
for a few embers
    Michael Ketchek
    Rochester, New York

full rain barrel
the sky
scrubbed clean
  Adelaide B. Shaw
  Somers, New York

  cardamom tea
  morning fog lifts
  birds sunbathe
    Marjorie Pezzoli
    Spring Valley, California

    black shingles
    white driftwood
    weathered
      Gordon Clark
      Damariscotta, Maine

  on the valley floor
  fighting fire with fire
  controlled burn today
    Joseph N. Schmidt, Jr.
    Alameda, California

made of stardust not shining
    Nancy Orr[11]
    Lewiston, Maine

earthworms
i breathe with my steps
between
    Kati Mohr[12]
    Nürnberg, Germany

    stone angel
    tilting her ear
    toward birdsong
        Kimberly Kuchar
        Austin, Texas

more than
silver and gold...
a teary eye
    Kendra E. Shaw
    San Diego, California

glowing mesquite
a prairie falcon
minding its business
    John Budan
    Newberg, Oregon

    a transistor radio
    transitioning to rust
    summer weeds
        Chad Lee Robinson[13]
        Pierre, South Dakota

        winter's blue sky
        the missing boy
        found
            Dian Duchin Reed[14]
            Soquel, California

    sheer canyon…
    old juniper's roots dangling
    in icy wind
        Al W. Gallia
        Lafayette, Louisiana

snow on the boats
winter pulls silence
from the sea
    Glenn C. Coats
    Carolina Shores, North Carolina

    our skiff's drift into a merganser's whistle
        Jo Balistreri[15]
        Waukesha, Wisconsin

        the empty chair
        by an open door
        meadow sweet
            Jennifer Thiermann
            Glenview, Illinois

      morning winds—
      a spider web fills
      with dandelion seeds
          Joseph P. Wechselberger
          Browns Mills, New Jersey

creeping sepia
a dog that outran
the wind
    Alan Summers[16]
    England

    Around soldiers neck
    blue ribbon, gold Minerva
    Medal of Honor
        Jason Scott Wallace
        Sherman Oaks, California

        Raven—
        the dark shadow
        that stole the sun
            Gil Jackofsky
            San Marcos, California

    for a second, all's well–
    washed silverware
    back in the drawer
        Robert Lowes[17]
        Saint Louis, Missouri

draining the bottle
the blazing log
collapses
    Rob Scott[18]
    Victoria, Australia

    October moon
    the garden orb's
    mercury web
        Theresa Mormino
        Hot Springs, Arkansas

        their names
        forgotten in dirt
        all the unmarked graves
            Mihan Han
            Richmond Hill, Ontario

    wind whistling—
    retaping the spine
    of my dictionary
        Edward J. Rielly
        Westbrook, Maine

water drops from the surfboard another divorce
    Scott Glander
    Glenview, Illinois

quiet conversations
dusk turns on
a streetlight
    Shawn Blair[19]
    Cohoes, New York

one drop of dew
on the basswood leaf's tip
the taste of hot days
    Elizabeth Hazen
    Williston, Vermont

a bloom of rust
on the hoe blade
pasture ironweed
    Meredith Ackroyd
    Afton, Virginia

long-tailed ichneumon wasp hold your breath
    Randy Brooks
    Taylorville, Illinois

    one tree stirs
    in a wind others seem
    not to feel
        David Cashman
        Providence, Rhode Island

        a burning log
        escapes the hearth
        winter stars
            Helen Ogden
            Pacific Grove, California

    delicate snowfall
    the words he chooses
    to tell her he cares
        Wanda Cook
        Hadley, Massachusetts

long married
he slowly stokes the fire
and it catches
    Roberta Beary[20]
    Ireland

    deep in the forest
    sound of rain continues
    long after it stops
        Beth Howard
        Cheyenne, Wyoming

        chinook wind
        he unbuttons
        her blouse
            Dave Reynolds
            Colorado Springs, Colorado

      just shy of a full moon blind date
        Jackie Maugh Robinson
        Las Vegas, Nevada

reflected
on rippling water
clapboard siding
> *Henry Brann*
> *Philadelphia, Pennsylvania*

morning mist
rising with the sun
yellow butterfly
> *Dennise Aiello*
> *Benton, Louisiana*

year's end—
beyond the cloud mass
a thickness of stars
> *Billie Wilson*
> *Juneau, Alaska*

yellow gorse
the path only a rabbit
can find
> *Thomas Chockley*
> *Plainfield, Illinois*

nose to tail
rainbow koi
making their own river
   Mike Fainzilber
   Israel

   partly cloudy
   one walkway to the sea
   lavender meadows
      Inas Asfari
      Oak Creek, Wisconsin

      ethereal song
      hermit thrush
      on the fire road
         Marilyn Gehant
         San Jose, California

     wind
     through the aspens…
     speaking of rain
        Dan Curtis
        Victoria, British Columbia

kitchen sink romance
the draining glasses full
of rainbows
  David J. Kelly
  Ireland

  night time
  the soothing sound
  of bathwater
    Patricia Harvey[21]
    East Longmeadow, Massachusetts

    a smell
    drifting by
    his apology
      Mike Montreuil
      Ottawa, Ontario

   New Year's Eve
   I cast my fortune
   in lead
    Charles Trumbull[22]
    Santa Fe, New Mexico

reaching out
once in a while —
Northern Lights
    Luce Pelletier
    Brossard, Quebec

summer
muscle memory
of a paper plane
    Fay Aoyagi
    San Francisco, California

cloud hands
over the mountains
breathing in…breathing out
    Lillian Nakamura Maguire[23]
    Whitehorse, Yukon

flame lily
my tongue parting
her lips
    Bryan Rickert
    Bellville, Illinois

old mining town
vying with the moon
the abandoned craters
    Madhuri Pillai
    Melbourne, Australia

    scent of the earth—
    salamander's
    Cretaceous nose
        Akihiko Hayashi
        Osaka, Japan

        goosebumps –
        in my breast pocket
        rose quartz
            Neal Whitman
            Pacific Grove, California

    gas-soaked wood
    the matchstick carves
    a hole in the night
        Ravi Kiran
        India

changing the em dash
to an ellipsis...
cherry blossoms
   Antoinette Cheung
   Vancouver, British Columbia

   writing in the wind
   the looping descent
   of a quail feather
     Margaret Tau
     New Bern, North Carolina

      new green leaf shadows
      paper her bedroom wall
      convalescence
        Margaret Chula
        Portland, Oregon

    pay day
    shirt pockets
    full of plums
      Billy Guerriero
      Littleton, Colorado

secret wedding
she throws her bouquet
to the wind
    Alvin B. Cruz[24]
    Philippines

        dawn in every dew drop a garden
            Mary Arnold
            Asheville, North Carolina

            rings around the raindrop—
            pockets
            full of pond
                Pegi Deitz Shea
                Vernon-Rockville, Connecticut

        an old woman
        dreams of childbirth
        solstice rain
            Dianne Garcia
            Seattle, Washington

winter morning
clouds parting ways
for more clouds
    Ben Gaa[25]
    St. Louis, Missouri

    sunset
    the variegated shades
    of mourning
        Carol Judkins[26]
        Carlsbad, California

        falling feather
        the air between
        my thumb and fingers
            Pat Davis[27]
            Concord, New Hampshire

    cry of a loon
    night shifting feathers
    beneath silver moon
        Frances Farrell
        Coon Rapids, Minnesota

the percent
of the body that is gold
dying warbler
    Sarah Metzler[28]
    Marion Center, Pennsylvania

    uncoiling the hose—
    water meant
    for last year's garden
        C.R. Manley
        Bellevue, Washington

        end of winter
        the way she trims her baby's
        memory bonsai
            Michael Dudley[29]
            Chatham, Ontario

    June drizzle
    the weight
    of so little
        Sam Bateman[30]
        Everett, Washington

after autumn leaves snow
   Carly Siegel Thorp
   Sterling, Massachusetts

   for my father...
   to the winter sun
   funeral bells toll
      Sean O'Connor
      County Tipperary, Ireland

      snow squalls —
      an amaryllis trumpets
      its defiance
         Sheila Sondik
         Bellingham, Washington

   windswept slopes
   ignite into stars —
   wild camas
      Karin Hedetniemi
      Victoria, British Columbia

steady downpour
the long and short
of earthworms
    Frank Hooven[31]
    Morrisville, Pennsylvania

    A full rotation
    Why mark the unchanging?
    The sparrows don't care.
        Jodi King
        Victor, New York

        the hazy line
        between dark and light
        autumn clouds
            Eric Arthen
            Worthington, Massachusetts

    corium
    these yearbooks
    still radioactive
        Joshua St. Clare
        New Freedom, Pennsylvania

autumn fog
rolling over the field
a raven's call
    Marianne Sahlin
    Sweden

prayer flags
tattered or new
the same wind
    Sarah Paris
    Santa Rosa, California

oak trees rising
from old church ruins —
voices in the wind
    Jacob D. Salzer[32]
    Vancouver, Washington

wrens rustle about
the bare maple
copper leaves
    Andrea Vlahakis
    Woodbury, Connecticut

sangre de cristo moonrise
the silhouettes
of scorched ponderosas
  Alanna C. Burke
  Santa Fe, New Mexico

  grandma's fall
  the metallic taste of blood
  she remembers
    Sandra St-Laurent
    Whitehorse, Yukon

    windswept field
    cannon wheels roll
    no more
      Paul Kulwatno
      Falls Church, Virginia

   disaster tourist
   Geiger counter clicks, clicks
   three-Eyed Susan
     JL Huffman
     Blue Ridge Mountains, North Carolina

Spring rain
outside the shelter
bubbles in the gutter
    Gail Greenwood
    Basking Ridge, New Jersey

    cherry blossoms
    billowy and billowing
    storm clouds
        Dean Summers
        Renton, Washington

        squabbling neighbors
        the sound of competing birdsong
            Jennifer Isham
            Delray Beach, Florida

    an average light…
    finding gold
    in the stubble
        Tony Williams
        Glasgow, Scotland

ocean lookout
finding the still point
already occupied
  Kathryn Bold[33]
  Trabuco Canyon, California

  fireworks—
  the lone firefly
  in an open jar
    Randall Herman
    Victoria, Texas

    a little less
    of everything
    winter moss
      Hans C. Dringenberg
      Kingston, Ontario

  a little bit of winter
  slipping in through the cracks
  a field mouse
    Rick Jackofsky
    Rocky Point, New York

bees in the lavender
particles that emerge
from a cloud of quarks
    J. Zimmerman
    Santa Cruz, California

    my shadow
    on the ski slope
    mare's tails in the blue
        Marcyn Del Clements
        Claremont, California

        sand dune
        the tracks of a bird
        lift in the wind
            Lorraine Haig[34]
            Australia

    desert winds
    a pinwheel spinning
    in the descansos
        Terri L. French
        Huntsville, Alabama

Beach combing
Looking for perfection
Smooth red sea glass
   William Thomas
   Henderson, Nevada

   a sprinkle of pixie dust in my teacup a lover
      Corine Timmer
      Faro, Portugal

   a gray strain
   a youthful crown
   auburn hair
      Patricia Cruzan
      Fayetteville, Georgia

   gray sky overhead
   winter's rain falls…
   candy-cane lights
      LaMon Brown
      Birmingham, Alabama

hail storm
waiting for what
she has to say next
    Lee Strong, OF
    Rochester, New York

rain-bent light
I teach the dog
to wait
    Genevieve Wynand[35]
    Coquitlam, British Columbia

growing
a stalactite…
the tears I've shed
    Julie Schwerin
    Sun Prairie, Wisconsin

polar night
the time it takes
the pills to work
    Jennifer Hambrick[36]
    Columbus, Ohio

a dappled nap beneath linden leaves whispering
    Mary McCormack
    La Grange Park, Illinois

    snowcapped mountains
    the sun's eyelid closing
    alpenglow
        Mark Hurtubise
        Spokane, Washington

        luminarias
        guide us to the Madonna—
        wind crackles brown bags
            Caroline A. LeBlanc
            Albuquerque, New Mexico

    winter stars
    I stir the beans
    in yesterday's soup
        Robert Witmer
        Tokyo, Japan

day after
two cardinals cavorting
in a fallen pine
    Raymond C. Roy
    Winston-Salemn, North Carolina

    alkali flies
    in a phalarope swirl
    Mono Lake
        Alison Woolpert[37]
        Santa Cruz, California

        a cool breeze
        stirs birch leaves on the pond
        a floating mobile
            Robert Erlandson
            Birmingham, Michigan

    wind advisory
    the passing gust
    of a promise
        Cynthia Anderson
        Yucca Valley, California

horizontal rain
she puts her dried flowers
in order
    Heather Lurie
    Rangiora, New Zeland

    genealogy
    searching for the stories
    left untold
        Brenda Lempp
        Madison, Wisconsin

        Deep pool's warm water
        Cuddles the weary body
        Soul slowly floats up
            Albert Micah Lewis
            Grand Rapids, Michigan

    toasting the brave new year
    with a cracked old cup
    kintsugi
        Charles Harmon
        Whittier, California

icy road
a coyote contorted
toward the forest
> *Agnes Eva Savich*
> *Austin, Texas*

    a few
    cling to what was
    winter elm
>> *Gregory Longenecker*[38]
>> *Pasadena, California*

        the burden
        of snowdrops
        covered with snow
>>> *Shelley Baker-Gard*
>>> *Portland, Oregon*

    New Year's Day—
    nothing on the page
    but the wind
>> *Munira Judith Avinger*
>> *Bellingham, Washington*

the hum of highways inhaling green meadows
    Rich Schilling[39]
    Saint Louis, Missouri

    a whiff of chlorine
    from the mercury cells—
    night shift
        Leanne Mumford
        New South Wales, Australia

        stained glass
        the spirit went in
        as color
            Michael J. Galkjo
            Houston, Texas

    dreaming in caveman we carbon date ourselves
        Peter Jastermsky[40]
        Morongo Valley, California

newborn's death date no wind to speak of
   Francine Banwarth[41]
   Dubuque, Iowa

   first Eucharist
   a scent of Old Spice
   on the elements
      Lew Watts
      Chicago, Illinois

                the bright light
            —on Euphrates pebbles
             crossing of warriors
                Bassem Al Kassem
                Syria

   Dad's birthday
   the garden gate creaks
   in the wind
      Wendy Toth Notarnicola
      Long Valley, New Jersey

broken clouds—
how long the cotton field
on my commute home
    Lenard D. Moore
    Raleigh, North Carolina

heat lightning
the ice settles
in my glass
    Cam M. Sato
    Williston, Vermont

monsoon
eyes
enlarged by the fishbowl
    Ross Neher
    New York, New York

out of time…
the life and death
of a summer rainbow
    Rebecca Drouilhet
    Picayune, Mississippi

cirrus bird
it stays longer
than a real one
   Mary Weidensaul
   Woodinville, Washington

high clouds mute the sun
snow covers the river trail
wren tracks lead the way
   Kathryn Poulsen Wood
   Bend, Oregon

final signature
sets her free
birdsong
   Merle Hinchee
   Cary, North Carolina

summer at the beach
shorebirds scratching the surface
to go deeper
   Karen Schlumpp
   Benicia, California

June thunder
the falling flames
of a hot air balloon
  Seretta Martin
  Santee, California

  sparks shooting
  off the lightning rod
  his answer
    Angela Terry
    Sequim, Washington

    slowly
    from the broken faucet
    one drop after another
      Judith Hishikawa
      Astoria, New York

  gluons
  breaking the bonds
  of sisterhood
    Colleen M. Farrelly
    Palmetto Bay, Florida

spring pond
more frogspawn
than yesterday
    John J. Han
    Manchester, Missouri

    a reflection
    in the vernal pool
    old growth oak
        Deb Koen[42]
        Rochester, New York

        Like a symphony
        Its movements change in tempo
        Whistling sonata
            Jennifer H. Monaghan
            Grant, Florida

    river valleys
    mountains
    in cottonwood bark
        Terranda King
        Albuquerque, New Mexico

unpaved lane
to the river bottom
three locked gates
>   *Johnnie Johnson Hafernik[43]*
>   *San Francisco, California*

>   trellis of wild
>   fuschia roses   snapdragons
>   flutter of scent
>   *Nancy Cavers Dougherty*
>   *Sebastopol, California*

the table
the exam's foundation
>   mind Pb'en
>   *Tom Hahney*
>   *Bellingham, Washington*

zen garden
he sheds stones
of self-importance
>   *Jocelyn Ajami*
>   *Chicago, Illinois*

somewhere between
actinium and zirconium
... me
   Alan S. Bridges
   Westford, Massachusetts

   beachcombing...
   the agates
   I remember
     Ce Rosenow
     Eugene, Oregon

      Gold and silver love
      Sparkle and shine like diamonds
      Who needs carbon rocks
        Ann Catanzariti
        Amesbury, Massachusetts

    the grain of quartz
    stuck to my thumb
    radio silence
      Aidan Castle
      Tacoma, Washington

exchange of vows…
every pause filled
by a goldfinch
    Tanya McDonald
    Happy Valley, Oregon

    new moon
    even nostalgia
    ain't what it used to be
        Edward Cody Huddleston
        Baxley, Georgia

        closer to forgiveness *lepidoptera*
            Kat Lehmann[44]
            Guilford, Connecticut

      firelight
    reading love letters
      for the last time
        Stephanie Story
        Corsicana, Texas

gmo tomātoes tomätoes
    Christopher Patchel[45]
    Libertyville, Illinois

moonless night
the distant flaring
of surplus gas
    Lynn Edge[46]
    Tivoli, Texas

mammatus clouds glitching 1s and 0s
    P. H. Fischer[47]
    Vancouver, British Columbia

deep breath of spring
the empty space inside
the Big Dipper
    James A Paulson[48]
    Narberth, Pennsylvania

August heat   pitch pines reclaim abandoned train tracks
Fred Donovan
South Chatham, Massachusetts

sand between his toes
remembering
how to be a child
Robert A. Oliveira
Bonita Springs, Florida

dandelion tufts
float away
prairie's grandchildren
Betsy Hearne
Urbana, Illinois

the mockingbird too
falls silent...
cottonwood breeze
Robert Gilliland
Austin, Texas

ripe with winter
a hammock sways
cradling snow
    Janet McKeehan-Medina
    Larchmont, New York

weathered seeds
drift through the air
thoughts follow
    Reva Levin
    Boston, Massachusetts

the shallows —
death is not the end
it's the elements
    Robert Epstein
    Berkeley, California

Meditating on a star
  who can say
    we're not the same age
  Sylvia Forges-Ryan
  North Haven, Connecticut

Thanksgiving night
the light across the courtyard
looking back
    Robert Forsythe
    Annandale, Virginia

    worshippers bow heads
    beneath stained glass windows
    sun lights their prayers
        Sharon Lynne Yee
        Torrance, California

        parsing the weather
        no name
        for the season
            Lori Zajkowski
            New York, New York

    plum wine in winter—
    last drink
    in this life
        Connie Goodman-Milone
        Miami, Florida

grog wedged
into the porcelain clay
edge of discovery
    Vincent Peter DeFatta
    Fort Smith, Arkansas

sixth chemistry class
teacher yawning
in elements
    Tomislav Sjekloća
    Cetinje, Montenegro

hunting for treasures
in these leaves
the deer skull
    Barbara Robinette
    Viola, Arkansas

rusty typewriter
how many spaces after
a full stop
    Roberta Beach Jacobson
    Indianola, Iowa

ghosting along
with the river's laughter
red dragonflies
> *Nathaniel Tico*
> *San Francisco, California*

midwinter snowmelt the messy truth
> *Sharon Martina*
> *Warrenville, Illinois*

Serene shimmering,
Oblong shapes with silver lines—
"Bloop!" plopped the pebble.
> *Sydney Vance*
> *Lower Gwynedd, Pennsylvania*

the yearning
beneath my wife's silence
wind-capped waves
> *Chen-ou Liu*
> *Ajax, Ontario*

Mother's criticism
pouring more salt
into the soup
    Robin Palley
    Philadelphia, Pennsylvania

    dental cleaning
    how dirty
    my shoes are
        Pearl Pirie
        Alcove, Quebec

        All illicit love—
        report to the IRS?
        Asking for a friend.
            Mary Thompson
            Apple Valley, California

    i still avoid
    stepping on cracks –
    mother's day
        dana
        San Jose, California

the river meets the ocean
a small barrier
to lean on
Gary Hotham[49]
Scaggsville, Maryland

oxygen and carbon
life or death
in an empty bottle
Andy Felong
Redwood City, California

Like a bright shadow
Running ahead of me, beach
sand in the winter wind
Jimmy Jung
Falls Church, Virginia

three little words
not uttered...
a deeper silence
Tom Lyon Freeland
Edmonton, Alberta

winter storm
my husband retreats
to the den
    Michelle Ballou
    Bellingham, Washington

new moon
a white chrysanthemum
breaks the silence
    Joseph Robello
    Mill Valley, California

lightning strike
the scab comes off
in pieces
    Cherie Hunter Day
    Atherton, California

daybreak
my song disappears
in the fog
    Barbara Tate Sayre[50]
    Winchester, Tennessee

front porch steps
    Mom and I
        lifting the sun from darkness
Kathi Ashmore
Waunakee, Wisconsin

    Snow rolling downhill.
    White envelops a rodent:
      Sly catastrophe.
        Soap Robinson
        New York, New York

      no one cutting in
      the dancers ever whirl
      two h's, one o
        David Neal Greenwood
        Basking Ridge, New Jersey

    solar-powered
    wings flapping
    pink flamingo
      Renie Newlon
      Albuquerque, New Mexico

water lily
drop after drop rolling
down her cheek
    Alex Fyffe
    Stafford, Texas

dandelion clock
always knows when it's time
to let go
    Garry Gay
    Santa Rosa, California

woodpecker knocking
on an old persimmon tree—
I open my door
    Daniel A. Zehner
    Woodstown, New Jersey

watering
a new desk plant
layoffs
    David Grayson
    Alameda, CA

pointillism
solving the mystery
in your eyes
    Ronald K. Craig
    Battavia, Ohio

    great-grandpa
    a blank domino
    in the boneyard
        Patricia McKernon Runkle
        Mendham, New Jersey

        beach sand—
        pitted
        by the storm
            Steven H. Greene
            Haddon Township, New Jersey

    between pages —
    black on white
    a crushed ant
        Veera Rajaratnam
        Franklin, Tennessee

the air
within and without you
bamboo flute
    Scott Wiggerman[51]
    Albuquerque, New Mexico

inside the wind the rain inside the tree
    Kathryn Liebowitz
    Groton, Massachusetts

Across the field,
all the neighbor's lights are on.
Saying goodbye.
    M. Brian Kelly
    Union, Maine

spring quickening
i spill my secrets
to the new moon
    Margie Gustafson[52]
    Lombard, Illinois

all the light
of a boyhood summer
first firefly
    Lee Hudspeth[53]
    Hermosa Beach, California

continental divide
the antlers of a bull moose
fill with sun
    Eric Sundquist
    Batesville, Virginia

the garden gnome
denies unplugging
the neon buddha
    Nika
    Alberta, Canada

late summer creek
a small leaf floats beyond
its reflection of home
    Michael Kitchen
    Chesterfield, Michigan

at the table
saving a place for
Ununennium
    Kathabela Wilson
    Pasadena, California

    early thaw
    the scent of peonies
    as her hair falls out
        Adele Evershed
        Wilton, Connecticut

        full moon
        on a platform of clouds
        political promises
            Antoinette Libro
            Saint Augustine, Florida

    doomed love:
    one carbon-based
    one silicon
        David Oates
        Athens, Georgia

flood waters
wind whipped froth
from who knows what
   Susan Spooner
   Victoria, British Columbia

   ruminating
   the mind whirs in shades of black
   awaiting a breath
      CJ Korisky
      Westborough, Massachusetts

      The rain hits my face.
      Thunder is loud, yet for me—
      It is oh so quiet.
         Lucien Petri
         Fort Collins, Colorado

   storm moon
   wind-chill ten below
   her last lie
      Susan Godwin
      Madison, Wisconsin

krypton, she said...
our neighbor protects
her future honeygold
    Lorraine A Padden
    San Diego, California

lifting up the sunlight seedlings
    Ann K. Schwader[54]
    Westminster, Colorado

the algorithms
of heliotropism—
ripe tomato
    Rick Clark
    Seattle, Washington

magnolia petals
a stray dog laps up
the sun
    Theresa A. Cancro
    Wilmington, Delaware

emissions rise
memorizing the scent
of April snow
  Sharon R. Wesoky
  Meadville, Pennsylvania

  fig tree buds
  begin to swell
  the question in his eyes
    Sharon Rhutasel-Jones
    Los Ranchos, New Mexico

    Bumble bee hovers
    Wild flowers dance here on wind
    Center of all things
      Belinda Seiger
      Princeton, New Jersey

  almost light
  walking away from work
  this spring evening
    Shasta Hatter[55]
    Portland, Oregon

vacuum
waiting to be filled
the diagnosis is …
 Ann Penton
 Green Valley, Arizona

another blursday
so much comes to me, then leaves
dark sky, silence—love
 Ellen Lord
 Charlevoix, Michigan

elements of surprise
and predictability—
the final act
 Barbara Fink
 Mountain View, California

Gaia's little joke
robin's egg blue sky
sleet on my lashes
 Michael Flanagan
 Woodbury, Minnesota

windswept landscape
a crow follows me
into my dream
    Larry Gust
    Lakefield, Minnesota

    sleet in the air…
    my son adds a Hershey's bar
    to Dad's coffin
        Michael Dylan Welch
        Sammamish, Washington

        One flowing ember
        carried in a fennel stalk,
        Olympian hearth
            Jennifer Howse
            Cold Spring, New York

    A loon's lonely cry
    Steaming coffee in a mug
        Glorious sunrise
        Keith Stevenson
        Ballwin, Missouri

another day
faces of itinerants
in the winter sun
   Jon Hare
   Falmouth, Massachusetts

snow crunch
the goal is the path
the path, the goal
   W. Jack Petersen
   Rochester, New York

the box is fuller
than she wanted it to be
more to leave behind
   Marilyn J. Wolf
   Fishers, Indiana

northern twilight
we quarter the buck
until sunrise
   Bruce H. Feingold
   Berkeley, California

starry night
peach stains
on my white blouse
    Haeja K. Chung
    East Lansing, Michigan

    Shadows painted
    on the street by a late
    afternoon sun
        Roberta Brown
        Royal Oak, Michigan

        sunrise sea water swirls his ashes at my ankles
            Margaret Walker[56]
            Lincoln, Nebraska

    melting snow…
    removing the embryo
    from the nitrogen tank
        Stella Pierides
        Germany

winter walk
dendrites stripped of
connections
    Colette Kern
    Southold, New York

    copper moon
    the taste of ash
    between us
        Christine Horner
        Lafayette, California

        rain against the windows
        difficult decisions
            John Paul Ciarrocchi
            Madison, Maine

    six years gone today —
    the school bus
    makes its last stop
        Joan Cheng
        Boulder, Colorado

sunset
flowers on her frock
still warm
   himānshu vyās
   Rajasthan, India

   mother's quilt
   each stitch a story
   unwritten
      Jone Rush MacCulloch
      Happy Valley, Oregon

      lost buttons
      the collecting of them
      a childhood game
         Vera Constantineau
         Copper Cliff, Oregon

     Kudzu covered
         Honeysuckle vines
     Shortness of breath
        Michael K. Smith
        Knoxville, Tennessee

starry night...
every known atom
in concert
   Jeffrey Ferrara
   Worcester, Massachusetts

painting the sea
she lets the water do
what water does
   Mimi Ahern

beneath folded hands
rise and fall of belly breath
ducks float just so
   Marsha Stern
   Bellow Falls, Vermont

where pebble ripples end if I weren't an I
   Lisa Gerlits
   Silverton, Oregon

red orange poppy
from the doorway
I can't see the dust
  Marylyn Burridge
  Albuquerque, New Mexico

  high winds
  sawed tree stumps
  line county roads
    Janice Munro
    Odessa, Ontario

    surprise storm
    no protection from
    the elements
      Renee Londner
      Prospect, Connecticut

   waning summer
   sometimes prayer
   is not enough
     Amy Losak
     Teaneck, New Jersey

vapours & viruses
the shadows of things
I can't see
    kjmunro
    Whitehorse, Yukon

    The one red tree amongst the greens
    A harbinger
    In a cold wind
        Henry Kellogg
        North Pomfret, Vermont

        My landfill is full
        it won't hold one more regret,
            yet I pile them on
        Philip Kenney
        Portland, Oregon

    the first orange
    across an empty farm
    silence
        Roy Kindelberger
        Edmonds, Washington

night passiflora
sounds of scurrying mice
    sweet fog
    William Vlach
    San Francisco, California

    fresh cut grass
    through an open window —
    first grandchild
        George Skane
        Georgetown, Massachusetts

        dandelions
        out loud
        between stones
            Ryoko M. Suzuki
            Shiga, Japan

        nanoparticles this tree's and mine
            Vicki McCullough[57]
            Vancouver, British Columbia

looking up
an old friend
winter moon
> *Mark Forrester*
> *Hyattsville, Maryland*

    all night rain
    a dry space
    where lovers parked
> *LeRoy Gorman*[58]
> *Napanee, Ontario*

        compound
        the chemistry
        between us
> *Didimay Dimacali*
> *Norwalk, California*

     an eternity
     of one night stands
     Tanabata
> *Dyana Basist*
> *Santa Cruz, California*

snowdrifts…
snowflakes my tongue
missed
    Richard Bruns[59]
    Napa, California

    leaden clouds
    pressing on steel seas
    winter's weight
        Gregory M. Wittkopp
        Pleasant Ridge, Michigan

        Unspoken moments
            A long history with much
            Forgotten for good.
        Rita Bennett
        Mullica Hill, New Jersey

    large boulders
    tumbling into the gardens
    my boundaries
        Adèle Weers
        Zürich, Switzerland

a trajectory of crows bending the bomb cyclone
Susan Yavaniski[60]
Cohes, New York

hard rain
letting her go
for the second time
Kevin Valentine
Mesquite, Texas

higher than this heat
winter waits among the peaks
summertime snow
Ashlyn Ohm
Lonsdale, Arkansas

hugging
in different directions
tectonic plates
John S. Green
Bellingham, Washington

Easter afternoon
snowdrops still bloom
in the sun
  Ellen Grace Olinger[61]
  Oostburg, Wisconsin

  compost pile…
  the melting snow
  uncovers Jack-o-lantern seeds
    Barbara Feehrer
    Westford, Massachusetts

    sun and clouds
    this first day of spring
    breaks even
      Tom Painting
      Atlanta, Georgia

  for a time we live
  in each other's touch
  chrysalis skin
    Michele Root-Bernstein
    East Lansing, Michigan

first light
shapes the darkness
hatsuhinode
   Deborah Burke Henderson[62]
   Ashland, Massachusetts

   silent daybreak
   the burnt pine's shadow
   keeps growing
      Almila Dükel[63]
      Muğla, Türkiye

      Bonnieux sunshine
      ~ grapevines wander
         far from home
         Maggie Roycraft
         Morristown, New Jersey

   Western Wall
   all day all night
   the sparrows
      Ryland Shengzhi Li
      Arlington, Virginia

the clear stream
air turning
aspen leaves
 Thomas Festa
 Highland, New York

 gone as soon
 as the sun hits it
 killer frost
  Linda Papanicolaou
  Stanford, California

  first snow. . .
  waiting a while
  to shovel
   Jim Laurila
   Florence, Massachusetts

  frozen trough
  I cup the warm breath
  of my horse
   Debbie Strange[64]
   Winnipeg, Manitoba

garden pebbles
each holds the silence
of its mountain
    Katherine Raine
    Central Otago, New Zeland

the drip drip drip
of millennia
worry stone
    Peggy Hale Bilbro
    Huntsville, Alabama

the Rio Grande
trickles down
to a misnomer
    Caroline Giles Banks
    Bloomington, Minnesota

back to the bluffs
of my childhood
1-Mississippi
    Donna Bauerly
    Dubuque, Iowa

sandstone cliff
soft tones rising
with the heat
    Celia Stuart-Powles
    Tulsa, Oklahoma

    sunbreak
    the way the water gathered
    on the dry soil
        Daniel Robinson
        Hoover, Alambama

        divining rod
        a twitch away
        from a wish
            Steve Bahr
            Roseburg, Oregon

    aftermath
        an empire of dust
    devils
    Lev Hart[65]
    Calgary, Alberta

i look up
surprised you've come again
spring rain
    Jeffrey Walthall
    Fairfax, Virginia

river pebbles
learning how to be
like water
    Deborah Karl-Brandt
    Bonn, Germany

neap tide
all my memories
seep into sand
    William Scott Galasso[66]
    Laguna Woods, California

a gull going
the other way
summer sea
    Michael Fessler
    Kanagawa-Ken, Japan

bees buzzing
beneath the hammock
hypnagogia
    Rick Tarquinio
    Bridgeton, New Jersey

    diversity
    in the neighborhood...
    Shih Tzu owners mingle
        Charlotte Digregorio[67]
        Winnetka, Illinois

        gulp!
        our resident bullfrog
        swallows a swallow
            Henry W. Kreuter
            Lebanon, New Jersey

    hummingbird
    where the feeder
        was
        Peter Meister
        Charlottesville, Virginia

blue planet
the depth
of our dream to fly
 Amelia Cotter[68]
 Chicago, Illinois

  hike of a lifetime
  between two trees
  arachnid crossing
   Katherine Gotthardt
   Bristow, Virginia

    footprints in the sand
    the tide turning
    our story
     Cyndi Lloyd
     Riverton, Utah

  June pears
  a thousand thumb-sized
  possibilities
   David Chandler
   Chicago, Illinois

wetlands
returning to the same spot
again and again
    Michael Henry Lee
    Saint Augustine, Florida

    lantern light
    the river slips
    through our fence
        Barbara Snow[69]
        Eugene, Oregon

        morning woods
        some of last night's rain
        falls on me
            Tim Cremin
            Andover, Massachusetts

    hollowed redwood
    became a two-man shelter
    blinding rainstorm
        Barth H. Ragatz
        Fort Wayne, Indiana

late autumn
one last nod
sunflower
> *Maureen Lanagan Haggerty*
> *Madison, New Jersey*

cold rain
a hawk has the hedgerow
to itself
> *Lesley Anne Swanson*
> *Coopersburg, Pennsylvania*

one crisp red leaf
cradled in the lavender
fall's artistry
> *Dorothy Peers*
> *Walnut Creek, California*

shortening days
the fish that ignored my fly
snatched by an eagle
> *James Zemke*
> *Cambodia*

autumn traffic
a line of leaves
drifts downstream
    Jay Friedenberg
    Sleepy Hollow, New York

    soft sell
    all diamonds set
    in rose, white or yellow
        Christine Wenk-Harrison
        Lago Vista, Texas

        creaking roots—
        our pear tree tunnels its way
        to the water pipes
            Ruth Esther Gilmore
            Hannover, Germany

    missing
        the
            house
                mudslide
  Marci McGill
  Cincinnati, Ohio

mice —
they may
or may not be there
    Laurie Wilcox-Meyer
    Asheville, North Carolina

    Lascaux Cave
    safe from the elements
    animal magic
        Mariam Kirby
        Tyler, Texas

        raindrops
        on the field stones
        a spattering of tree frogs
            Lysa Collins
            White Rock, British Columbia

      password protected
      chick-a-dee-dee-dee
      opens the day
          Teri White Carns
          Anchorage, Alaska

hydrangea blooms
under the shrine. . .
water sprinkle
>   *Joan Canby*
>   *Garland, Texas*

three generations
in Sunday best
blackberries ripen
>   *L. Teresa Church*
>   *Durham, North Carolina*

afternoon tea
the mix of colors
in our conversation
>   *j rap[70]*
>   *Albuquerque, New Mexico*

at the altar
a cherry petal falls
from her sole
>   *brett brady[71]*
>   *Haiku, Hawaii*

between us another nail in the coffin
    Don Baird[72]
    Wake Forest, North Carolina

    another shooting…
    the soft thud
    of a leaf
        Miriam Borne
        Montgomery, Alabama

        Streetwise feral cat
        running from callous kids
        didn't see the car.
            Lorraine Rose
            Brewster, New York

    first day of spring
    my dog's ashes
    in the mailbox
        Robyn Hood Black
        Travelers Rest, South Carolina

pale birch leaf
on melting snow
    —tree's long shadow
     Cynthia Brackett-Vincent
     Farmington, Maine

    vernal equinox
    the windows stained
    with winter
       Jacob Blumner
       Flint, Michigan

        sprays of sunshine
        in the cold April rain
        forsythia
          Susan Farner
          Urbana, Illinois

    meandering river
    the time it takes
    for goslings
      Jill Lange[73]
      Cleveland Heights, Ohio

falling snow
everything a blur
but the cardinal
    Patricia Wakimoto[74]
    Gardena, California

    deep thought—
    underground stream
    flows through the forest
        Susan Lee Roberts
        Montesano, Washington

        a lonely whisper
        lost in a big house...
        light sleet
            Anna Cates
            Wilmington, Ohio

    flickering lights
    the nearest neighbor
    a mile away
        Allyson Whipple
        St. Louis, Missouri

heat dome
the walnut armoire's
muffled *krak*
  Connie Hutchinson
  Kirkland, Washington

  approaching storm —
  the slow rolling waves
  of tall grass
    Chris Langer
    Stephenville, Texas

    shockwaves Vulcan roar across the seas
      Bona M. Santos[75]
      Los Angeles, California

  tectonic shifts
  learning new ways to fill
  holes left by loss
    Claire Vogel Camargo[76]
    Austin, Texas

reeds edging the marsh blackbirds in bloom
    Ferris Gilli[77]
    Marietta, Georgia

holes in a lotus leaf
the width between
my eyes
    Gideon Young
    Chapel Hill, North Carolina

peony blossom
wafting in the evening breeze
sip of rosé
    Momoyo Capanna
    San Clement, California

if only
for this day
yellow daffodils
    John Quinnett
    Bryson City, North Carolina

golden spiral
a baby pepper
in my palm
    Jessica Allyson
    Ottawa, Ontario

        hot pink penstamen
        purveyor of fine spirits
        where bees go to drink
            Alice Mallory
            Ashland, Oregon

                hillside orange hues
                springtime poppies explode
                floral lava
                    Sandra Payne
                    Studio City, California

        days of rain
        purple gnaws its way
        out of a pansy
            Bill Deegan
            Ephrata, Pennsylvania

melting snow
on the library lawn
my book overdue
    Sari Grandstaff[8]
    Saugerties, NY

lilacs
she updates her will
to live
    Marilyn Powell
    Morristown, NJ

the next day
the turned earth
waits
    Perry L. Powell
    Snellville, Georgia

spring melt
an engorged tick
lets go
    Paul Hendricks
    Missoula, Montana

snowblower blades
clogged with leaves
the pending storm
> *Paul Cordeiro*
> *South Dartmouth, Massachusetts*

    I put my glasses on
    to see the fog
    more clearly
> *John Brehm*
> *Portland, Oregon*

        barn swallows chittering
                between highrises
           a dime at my feet
> *Marshall Hryciuk*
> *Etobicoke, Ontario*

    the weather channel
    a ladybug storms
    the TV screen
> *Luminita Suse[79]*
> *Gloucester, Ontario*

whole shells few and far between
focusing now
on the broken and still beautiful shards
    John Berkley
    Statesville, NC

    Butterfly flying ~
    Landing on my outstretched hand.
    Lightly it sits there!
        Aurore Leigh Barrett
        Las Vegas, Nevada

        Dew drops diamond glaze
        buzzing bee sipping nectar
        cricket leaping high
            Remona Winston
            Orlando, Florida

    summer social
    flitting from table to table
    the flies
        Karen DiNobile
        Norwalk, California

April downpour
a rising pool
of earthworms
    Lori Becherer
    Millstadt, Illinois

    plot twist
    volunteer tomatoes
    take over the yard
        Deborah P Kolodji
        Temple City, California

        churchyard bees in and out a pop can
            Hans Jongman[80]
            Welland, Ontario

        thunderstorm shadows slash the dying grass
            Pris Campbell
            Lake Worth, Florida

the approval of God
decaying atom
    Jerome Berglund
    Richfield, Minnesota

waiting to board
plastic palm fronds
wilting
    Warren Decker
    Izumi, Japan

distant thunder
the teal's reflection
fractured by cattails
    Kristen Lindquist
    Camden, Maine

left one sprinkler on one earth left
    Chuck Brickley[81]
    Daly City, California

Index of Poets

Meredith Ackroyd 20
Mimi Ahern 78
Dennise Aiello 23
Jocelyn Ajami 51
Bassem Al Kassem 46
Jessica Allyson 103
Cynthia Anderson 42
Fay Aoyagi 26
Mary Arnold 29
Eric Arthen 33
Inas Asfari 24
Kathi Ashmore 63
Joanna Ashwell 2
Marcie Flinchum Atkins 7
Susan B. Auld 4
Munira Judith Avinger 44
Shelley Baker-Gard 44
Steve Bahr 89
Don Baird 98
Jo Balistreri 17
Michele Ballou 62
Caroline Giles Banks 88
Francine Banwarth 46
Aurore Leigh Barrett 106
Dyana Basist 82
Sam Bateman 31
Donna Bauerly 88
Roberta Beary 22
Lori Becherer 107
Brad Bennett 8
Rita Bennett 83
John Berkley 106
Maxianne Berger 3

Jerome Berglund 108
Peggy Hale Bilbro 88
Robyn Hood Black 98
Shawn Blair 20
Jacob Blumner 99
Kathryn Bold 37
Miriam Borne 98
Cynthia Brackett-Vincent 99
brett brady 97
Henry Brann 23
John Brehm 105
Chuck Brickley 108
Alan S. Bridges 52
Valorie Broadhurst Woerdehoff 9
Randy Brooks 21
LaMon Brown 39
Roberta Brown 75
Richard Bruns 83
John Budan 16
Alanna C. Burke 35
Marylyn Burridge 79
Sondra J. Byrnes 13
Claire Vogel Camargo 101
Pris Campbell 107
Joan Canby 97
Theresa A. Cancro 70
Momoyo Capanna 102
Teri White Carns 96
Matthew Caretti 13
David Cashman 21
Aidan Castle 52
Ann Catanzariti 52
Anna Cates 100
Nancy Cavers Dougherty 51
David Chandler 92

Anette Chaney	5
Joan Cheng	76
Antoinette Cheung	28
Thomas Chockley	23
Margaret Chula	28
Haeja K. Chung	75
L. Teresa Church	97
John Paul Ciarrocchi	76
petro c. k.	9
Gordon Clark	14
Rick Clark	70
Tom Clausen	1
Glenn C. Coats	17
Lysa Collins	96
Vera Constantineau	77
Wanda Cook	21
Paul Cordeiro	105
Amelia Cotter	92
Ronald K. Craig	65
Tim Cremin	93
Alvin B. Cruz	29
Daniel Shank Cruz	12
Patricia Cruzan	39
Dan Curtis	24
dana	60
Pat Davis	30
Cherie Hunter Day	62
Juan Edgardo De Pascuale	1
Vincent Peter DeFatta	58
Warren Decker	108
Marcyn Del Clements	38
Bill Deegan	103
Charlotte Digregorio	91
Didimay Dimacali	82
Karen DiNobile	106

Fred Donovan 55
Hans C. Dringenberg 37
Rebecca Drouilhet 47
Michael Dudley 31
Almila Dükel 86
Lynn Edge 54
Robert Epstein 56
Eavonka Ettinger 10
Robert Erlandson 42
Adele Evershed 68
Mike Fainzilber 24
Susan Farner 99
Frances Farrell 30
Colleen M. Farrelly 49
Barbara Feehrer 85
Bruce H. Feingold 74
Andy Felong 61
Jeffrey Ferrara 78
Thomas Festa 87
Michael Fessler 90
Joan Fingon 7
Barbara Fink 72
P. H. Fischer 54
Michael Flanagan 72
Marylin Fleming 10
Denise Fontaine-Pincince 2
Sylvia Forges-Ryan 56
Robert Forsythe 57
Mark Forrester 82
Tom Lyon Freeland 61
Terri L. French 38
Jay Friedenberg 95
Alex Fyffe 64
Ben Gaa 30
William Scott Galasso 90

Michael J. Galkjo	45
Al W. Gallia	16
Dianne Garcia	29
Garry Gay	64
Marilyn Gehant	24
Lisa Gerlits	78
Ferris Gilli	102
Robert Gilliland	55
Ruth Esther Gilmore	95
Scott Glander	20
Susan Godwin	69
Kathy Goldbach	1
Connie Goodman-Milone	57
LeRoy Gorman	82
Katherine Gotthardt	92
Sari Grandstaff	104
David Grayson	64
John S. Green	84
Steven H. Greene	65
David Neal Greenwood	63
Gail Greenwood	36
Billy Guerriero	28
Larry Gust	73
Margie Gustafson	66
Johnnie Johnson Hafernik	51
Maureen Lanagan Haggerty	94
Tom Hahney	51
Lorraine Haig	38
Jennifer Hambrick	40
John J. Han	50
Mihan Han	19
Jon Hanzen	11
Jon Hare	74
Charles Harmon	43
Lev Hart	89

Penny Harter	13
Patricia Harvey	25
Shasta Hatter	71
Akihiko Hayashi	27
Elizabeth Hazen	20
Betsy Hearne	55
Karin Hedetniemi	32
Paul Hendricks	104
Deborah Burke Henderson	86
Randall Herman	37
Frank Higgins	9
Merle Hinchee	48
Judith Hishikawa	49
Christine Horner	76
Gary Hotham	61
Frank Hooven	33
Lee Hudspeth	67
JL Huffman	35
Edward Cody Huddleston	53
Mark Hurtubise	42
Connie Hutchinson	101
Beth Howard	22
Jennifer Howse	73
Marshall Hryciuk	105
Jennifer Isham	36
Gil Jackofsky	18
Rick Jackofsky	37
Roberta Beach Jacobson	58
Peter Jastermsky	45
Hans Jongman	107
Carol Judkins	30
Jimmy Jung	61
Deborah Karl-Brandt	90
Henry Kellogg	80
David J. Kelly	25

M. Brian Kelly 66
Philip Kenney 80
Colette Kern 76
Jill Kessler 11
Michael Ketchek 13
Howard Lee Kilby 4
Roy Kindelberger 80
Jodi King 33
Terranda King 50
Ravi Kiran 27
Mariam Kirby 96
Michael Kitchen 67
kjmunro 80
Deb Koen 50
Deborah P Kolodji 107
CJ Korisky 69
Henry W. Kreuter 91
Kimberly Kuchar 15
Paul Kulwatno 35
Monica Lajoie 10
Jill Lange 99
Chris Langer 101
Jim Laurila 87
Caroline A. LeBlanc 41
Michael Henry Lee 93
Kat Lehmann 53
Brenda Lempp 43
Reva Levin 56
Barrie Levine 4
Albert Micah Lewis 43
Ryland Shengzhi Li 86
Antoinette Libro 68
Kathryn Liebowitz 66
Kristen Lindquist 108
Chen-ou Liu 59

Cyndi Lloyd 92
Renee Londner 79
Gregory Longenecker 44
Ellen Lord 72
Amy Losak 79
Robert Lowes 18
Heather Lurie 43
Jone Rush MacCulloch 77
Patricia J. Machmiller 8
Lillian Nakamura Maguire 26
Annette Makino 8
Alice Mallory 103
C.R. Manley 31
Seretta Martin 49
Sharon Martina 59
Richard L. Matta 3
Jackie Maugh Robinson 22
Mary McCormack 41
Vicki McCullough 81
Tanya McDonald 53
Marci McGill 95
Janet McKeehan-Medina 56
Peter Meister 91
MJ Mello 11
Sarah Metzler 31
Kati Mohr 15
Beverly Acuff Momoi 3
Jennifer H. Monaghan 50
Mike Montreuil 25
Lenard D. Moore 47
Theresa Mormino 19
Wilda Morris 12
Marsh Muirhead 7
Leanne Mumford 45
Janice Munro 79

Nika 67
Ross Neher 47
Renie Newlon 63
Suzanne Niedzielska 2
Sean O'Connor 32
William O'Sullivan 9
David Oates 68
Helen Ogden 21
Ashlyn Ohm 84
Ellen Grace Olinger 85
Robert A. Oliveira 55
Nancy Orr 15
Roland Packer 1
Lorraine A Padden 70
Tom Painting 85
Robin Palley 60
Christa Pandey 8
Linda Papanicolaou 87
Sarah Paris 34
Christopher Patchel 54
James A Paulson 54
Sandra Payne 103
Dorothy Peers 94
Luce Pelletier 26
Ann Penton 72
W. Jack Petersen 74
Lucien Petri 69
Marjorie Pezzoli 14
Stella Pierides 75
Madhuri Pillai 27
Pearl Pirie 60
Marilyn Powell 104
Perry L. Powell 104
Kathryn Pumphrey 4
John Quinnett 102

Emily Rademacher	5
Barth H. Ragatz	93
Katherine Raine	88
Veera Rajaratnam	65
j rap	97
Dian Duchin Reed	16
Mike Rehling	6
Dave Reynolds	22
Sharon Rhutasel-Jones	71
Edward J. Rielly	19
Bryan Rickert	26
Joseph Robello	62
Susan Lee Roberts	100
Barbara Robinette	58
Chad Lee Robinson	16
Daniel Robinson	89
Soap Robinson	63
Michele Root-Bernstein	85
Maggie Roycraft	86
Lorraine Rose	98
Ce Rosenow	52
Raymond C. Roy	42
Patricia McKernon Runkle	65
Marianne Sahlin	34
Jacob D. Salzer	34
Bona M. Santos	101
Kelly Sargent	10
Cam M. Sato	47
Agnes Eva Savich	44
Barbara Tate Sayre	62
Michelle Schaefer	5
Judith Morrison Schallberger	6
Rich Schilling	45
Karen Schlumpp	48
Joseph N. Schmidt, Jr.	14

Ann K. Schwader	70
Julie Schwerin	40
Rob Scott	19
Belinda Seiger	71
Adelaide B. Shaw	14
Kendra E. Shaw	15
Pegi Deitz Shea	29
Michael Sheffield	12
Tomislav Sjekloća	58
George Skane	81
Michael K. Smith	77
Barbara Snow	93
Sheila Sondik	32
Lisa Sparaco	12
Susan Spooner	69
Joshua St. Clare	33
Sandra St-Laurent	35
Bonnie Stepenoff	5
Marsha Stern	78
Keith Stevenson	73
Stephanie Story	53
Debbie Strange	87
Lee Strong, OF	40
Celia Stuart-Powles	89
Alan Summers	18
Dean Summers	36
Eric Sundquist	67
Luminita Suse	105
Ryoko M. Suzuki	81
Lesley Anne Swanson	94
Eric Tanner	7
Rick Tarquinio	91
Margaret Tau	28
Angela Terry	49
Jennifer Thiermann	17

William Thomas 39
Mary Thompson 60
Carly Siegel Thorp 32
Richard Tice 6
Nathaniel Tico 59
Corine Timmer 39
Wendy Toth Notarnicola 46
Xenia Tran 2
Deborah Troner 11
Charles Trumbull 25
Kevin Valentine 84
Sydney Vance 59
William Vlach 81
Andrea Vlahakis 34
himānshu vyās 77
Patricia Wakimoto 100
Marilyn Appl Walker 6
Margaret Walker 75
Jason Scott Wallace 18
Diane Wallihan 3
Jeffrey Walthall 90
Lew Watts 46
Joseph P. Wechselberger 17
Adèle Weers 83
Mary Weidensaul 48
Michael Dylan Welch 73
Christine Wenk-Harrison 95
Sharon R. Wesoky 71
Allyson Whipple 100
Neal Whitman 27
Scott Wiggerman 66
Laurie Wilcox-Meyer 96
Tony Williams 36
Billie Wilson 23
Kathabela Wilson 68

Remona Winston 106
Robert Witmer 41
Gregory M. Wittkopp 83
Marilyn J. Wolf 74
Kathryn Poulsen Wood 48
Alison Woolpert 42
Genevieve Wynand 40
Susan Yavaniski 84
Sharon Lynne Yee 57
Gideon Young 102
Lori Zajkowski 57
Daniel A. Zehner 64
James Zemke 94
J. Zimmerman 38

Endnotes

1. *Noon: journal of the short poem*, Issue 20, October 2021
2. *The Bamboo Hut*, Issue One, 2023
3. *Presence* #75, March 2023
4. *Akitsu Quarterly*, Spring/Summer 2023
5. *Frogpond* 38.3, Autumn 2015
6. *Acorn* #29, fall 2012
7. *Modern Haiku* 41.1, 2010
8. *Triveni Haikai India*, August 9, 2022
9. *Failed Haiku*, Issue 87, February 2023
10. *Presence* #71, 2021
11. *Frogpond* 45:3, Autumn 2022
12. *Kingfisher* #6, October 2022
13. *Mariposa* #32, Spring/Summer 2015
14. Honorable Mention, The Robert Spiess Memorial Haiku Award Competition, 2022
15. *brass bell*, November 2022
16. *Presence* #71, 2021
17. *Presence* #75, March 2023
18. *Frogpond,* 45:2, Spring/Summer 2022
19. *tsuri-dōrō*, March/April 2023
20. *Lakeview International Journal of Literature and Arts*, 1.2, August 2013
21. *New England Letters*, July 2022
22. *The Snowman's Companion* (broadsheet, 2009)
23. *Moving Meditations*, edited by Lynne Jambor, 2021
24. *Prune Juice* # 38
25. *Blithe Spirit* 32.1
26. First verse in rengay, "Kaleidoscope", HSA rengay contest 2023, Honorable Mention
27. *Hedgerow* #121, Fall 2017
28. *Modern Haiku* 50:3
29. *Mayfly*, Winter 2023

30 *The Heron's Nest*, Vol.22, No. 3, 2020
31 *Shamrock* #42, Summer 2019
32 *Under the Bashō* 2023
33 *Frogpond 45*:2, spring/summer 2022
34 *Presence* #73
35 *The Heron's Nest* Volume XXIV, Number 1, March 2022
36 *Heliosparrow Poetry Journal*, 2 Oct. 2022
37 *Acorn* Spring 2023
38 *Modern Haiku* 54:2, 2023
39 *bones* 25
40 *Heliosparrow Poetry Journal*, November 2020
41 *Modern Haiku* 53.3
42 *Haiku Canada Review*, Winter 2020
43 *Modern Haiku* 53:2, Summer 2022
44 *Sonic Boom* (2020)
45 HaikuNow! 2013 contest
46 *The Heron's Nest* December 2016
47 *Kingfisher* #7
48 *Frogpond 25:1*, 2002
49 *Noon,* Summer 2022
50 *Blithe* Spirit 2021:3
51 *Paper Mountains: Seabeck Haiku Anthology 2021*
52 *Troutswirl* April 2023
53 *The Heron's Nest* 24:2, June 2022
54 *Frogpond* 45.1
55 *50 Haikus* #14, 2018
56 *Whiptail 4: humbled vessel*, August 2022
57 *Tidepools: Haiku On Gabriola*, Michael Dylan Welch (ed.). Pacific Rim Publishers, 2011
58 *Modern Haiku, 52:3*, Autumn 2021
59 *Akitsu Quarterly*, Winter 2017
60 *Whiptail 6: Cloudbreak,* February 2023
61 *Scarlet Dragonfly* #13, April 2023

62	*Chrysanthemum* #80, April 2023
63	*Modern Haiku* 54.1
64	1st Place, Sharpening the Green Pencil Haiku Contest, 2018
65	*haikuKATHA* #13, Nov. 2022
66	*Chrysanthemum* #30
67	*Haiku Canada Review*, Vol. 17, No. 1, February 2023
68	Golden Triangle's 2018 Golden Haiku Competition, March 2018
69	*The Heron's Nest*, Sept. 2009
70	*Stardust Haiku*, March 2023
71	Sakura Award 2010 Cherry Blossom Festival Haiku Contest
72	*Heliosparrow Poetry Journal*, 2023
73	*The Heron's Nest*, June 2019
74	*Geppo* (volume XLVII) Nov-Jan 2022; *Red Paper Parasols*, 2022
75	*Asahi Haikuist Network*, 21 October 2022
76	*Frameless Sky* #13
77	*Frogpond* 44:2
78	*The Mainichi Daily Haiku in English*, March 2, 2023
79	*Haiku Canada Review* 9:2, 2015
80	*SYZYGY*, 2022
81	*Whiptail 5: As the Now Takes Hold*, November 2022